BARTOSZ NOWICKI

Nowicki
2013

TEXT BY ANNIS ABRAHAM JNR, CARL CURTIS AND JAMES LEIGHTON

THE IMPOSSIBLE DREAM BY JAMES LEIGHTON

My love affair with Cardiff City started in April 1988, when my father took me to a crumbling, desolate, Ninian Park, to watch my first football match. On the day Cardiff emerged victorious, walloping local rivals, Newport County, 4-0. The result and performance led me to mistakenly believe I was on to a winner. My classmates could stick their Liverpool shirts. I was supporting the true glory team. Sadly, I wasn't to know that this type of barnstorming display was an aberration and that more often than not my new team would flatter to deceive.

Back then we were still the Bluebirds, we were playing in the old Division Four, and we were averaging gates of just 5,000. It was a far cry from what you see at Cardiff City today but it was magic. From the smell of Bovril wafting across the terraces, where fans were still allowed to stand, and able to generate an incredible atmosphere despite their small numbers, to the peeling Captain Morgan Rum advert emblazoned across the roof of the Bob Bank. It was those little things, rather than the goals scored by Stevenson, McDermott, Wimbleton and Ford, which have forever stayed in my mind. Of course, since then, for better or for worse, we have evolved into Vincent Tan's Red Dragons. We now play our home games in a state of the art, all-seater stadium, in front of an average crowd of 20,000. And rather than flounder in the basement of the Football League we are now strutting our stuff in the Premier League, the richest and glitziest sports league in the world, with fans stretching far and wide, from the Rhondda Valleys to Kuala Lumpur.

It has certainly been a remarkable journey, perhaps unmatched by any other football team in the UK for its sheer drama. Along the way we've seen the great side of football, the stuff that makes the trials and tribulations of being a fan worthwhile. We've seen the advent of the 'Ayatollah', Eddie May's Barmy Army, remarkable cup runs that have taken us to the FA and League Cup Finals, as well as a series of promotions sparked by the purchase of multi-million pound footballers. However, these good times have come at a considerable cost.

I've lost count of the amount of times the club has almost gone bust or ended up in court. Back in the 1980s, a financial crisis was triggered by something as simple as thieves stealing the ticket receipts following a cup tie against QPR. Since then our financial crises have been far more complicated, with stories involving cavalier chairman, off shore companies, the Inland Revenue and outlandish player contracts. As fans we've certainly gone through the mill and have wondered at times if our football club would see out the season, let alone concern ourselves with trivial matters such as promotion or relegation.

It was for those very reasons that a large proportion of the fan base neglected to vehemently protest when Vincent Tan pushed through the controversial rebrand last summer. Rather than riot, or wave the white flag, the approach taken by most City fans was conciliatory. The future of the club was said to be at stake and while 99% of Cardiff fans desperately wanted to remain in blue there was a chance that a raft of protests could see our billionaire chairman pull the plug, plunging us into administration in the process. Faced with this nightmare scenario, as Bart's fantastic pictures show, the fans continued to support the club in large numbers with the same passion and commitment as ever. Nothing was done which could take the team's eye off the ball. Much has been made of the professionalism and commitment displayed by Malky and the boys as they romped to the title but I think those same traits were also shown by the fans, who perhaps had more reason than any others to walk away when faced with such an unpalatable change.

While the season ended with one of the great moments in Cardiff City history, the pitch invasion sparked by our 0-0 draw with Charlton, which finally saw us clinch promotion, many fans still felt it could have been all the better if we had been playing in blue. Yet despite this tinge of regret the pictures of that famous night really emphasize that while colour and tradition are vital to a football club, the most important thing of all are its fans. Without the commitment and resilience of those thousands of fans who swamped the pitch Cardiff City would have gone under long ago.

So as we look forward to watching some of the world's great footballers grace the Cardiff City Stadium we should also take pride in the fact that the Premier League will finally be graced by some of the world's greatest fans, who give up considerable time, money, and energy to go wherever their football club demands. I'm not sure the Premier League will have ever seen the like of our fervent fan base. I know we will do ourselves proud.

As I gear myself up for at least one season in the promised land there is one thing I am looking forward to far more than the prospect of Manchester United coming to town, it is the chance to complete a journey that started 25 years ago, a chance to watch Cardiff City in the top flight alongside my father. We both thought we would never see the day, particularly after witnessing us lose 5-0 at home to Maidstone. I am sure we will both enjoy every minute of it, as will thousands of others, who are proud to support the mighty Cardiff City. I just hope we can soon have our cake and eat it, with us being a force in the top flight, backed to the hilt by our billionaire benefactor, and back to playing in blue.

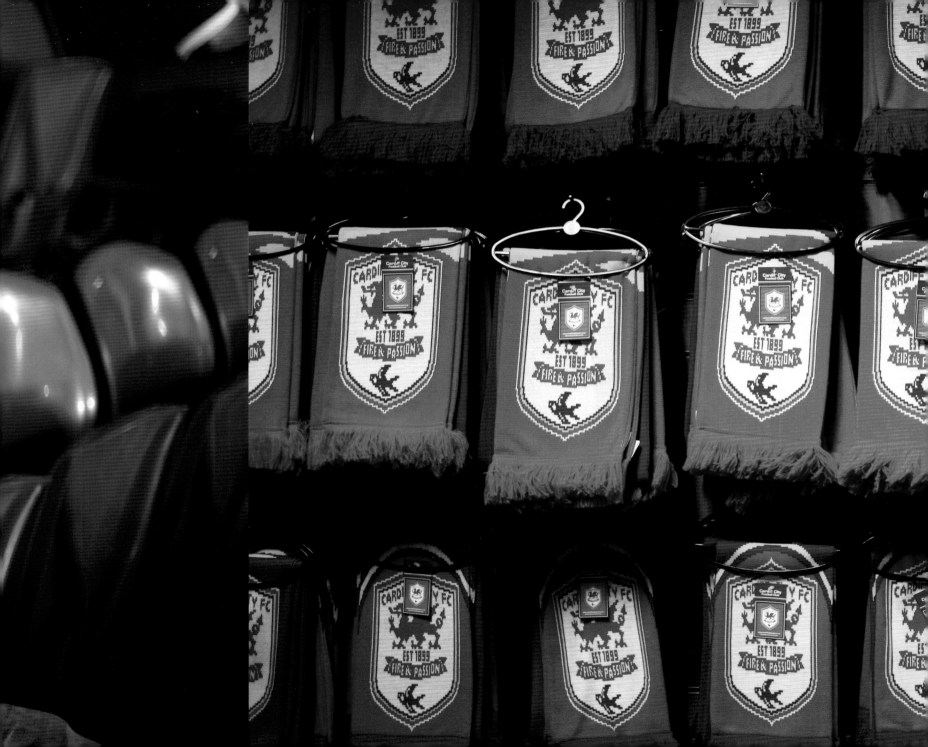

WE'LL ALWAYS BE BLUE BY ANNIS ABRAHAM JNR

The past 13 years have been nothing but success on the pitch for Cardiff City FC. We're always up there or thereabouts but it all suddenly changed and went weird in 2012.

In May that year we were travelling back from West Ham away, having just lost in the play-offs. We were all on the downer. I knew we would lose anyway after being beaten in the first leg. We were outplayed, the opposition were quality. West Ham were just too good for Cardiff.

On the coach home someone said 'Look on the website, Cardiff City will be rebranded, they are going to play in red and stripped of their identity.'

We didn't believe it, both Carl and I said 'It has to be a joke, no way; someone is just being an idiot.'

It would not happen to our club, Cardiff City.

Within 24 hours the club contacted me and asked me to attend a private meeting with them. I went along and there were 12 fans there in total. My god, they were on about it... Taking our badge away, taking the colour that has been here for over 100 years, our colour blue.

I was devastated.

They told us that if we didn't accept it, billionaire investor Vincent Tan wouldn't continue putting any more money in our club. The club officials in the meeting never said we'll go bust and be dead as people say, but we would probably go down a league and get ourselves in trouble. Few went all for it, (I couldn't believe it) and they actually said, 'Yes, yes, we should love that man'.

The majority in the room on that day stood firm and said 'no'. We then went away and thought about what was said. Next thing, the club called us all back a few days later and said there has been uproar. Tan will not continue to invest and will put in no more money and you can keep your colour.

For a few minutes I thought 'My god there will be no club', it was the way they said it. Carl and I looked at each other. 'Oh my god, no club...' Then I started to think about it. There will always be the club. As long as we've got a fan base and the hard core fans, we will always have a club. We can stand up to this man.

I was stunned by certain fans who were in the meeting... They went outside, straight to the media and told the fans to back Tan, told the media they agreed with it. That stunned and hurt me, that fellow fans that I have known for years, were all for Tan. They had their reasons, their beliefs, but I don't agree with them. That's the way the summer had gone. It hurt me beyond. All that summer I couldn't get over it.

I flew back from Spain to go to Cardiff versus Huddersfield. I came back with my eldest daughter who was 12 and I thought I have never worn a football shirt in my life for a football match. I just used to watch dressed as a casual. Some people said 'you have never worn blue before.' It doesn't matter what I wore before, I am used to what I look at on the pitch and what I watched was my beloved Cardiff City in blue and I am blue through and through. So I turned up that night, in the blue top, not knowing what to expect, hoping that the majority of the crowd will be blue...

When I'd been away there had been an event for 7000 fans at the stadium and there were thousands buying and wearing red. People were holding up the red, more people were showing their red. Going around the stadium many paraded in red. You have to remember we've gone from a crowd of three to four thousand in the last 12 years to crowds of twenty thousand plus. The majority of these people, they were not there over the years, so it's easy for them to go with the change to red. We're Blue, as far as I am concerned. So when people see older people and think, 'if they can change, maybe we should!' No way.

The few thousand of the hard core fans, 90% of them believe in blue, but we are in the minority. We are outnumbered by 10 to 1. You only have to look at the waiting list for the season tickets now. It just reached 10000... So many people are not bothered

So I turned up for that game against Huddersfield. My little daughter and I were gobsmacked. 'My god daddy, who do they support?' I even had a wind up with the stewards and said 'Quick, quick, there are away fans downstairs!' They all went down. 'Where, Annis?' 'They are everywhere!' 'Where?' They were asking.

I said 'Look at all of them in red'. Huddersfield fans then took the mick out of us and it's going to happen at every game this season. I was devastated. I left this game 5 minutes early... It took me 17 games just to clap them. I was broken that season. What turned out to be probably one of our greatest seasons for 50 years, to me it was spoiled, tarnished.

Vincent Tan could be the greatest chairman in our history, but he is not. Because he took away our identity, whether people like it or not we are Cardiff City and we are blue, we are the Bluebirds.

The final straw came when he went too far before the game against Brighton at home. Helped by people within our club, he gave away 23000 red scarves. I left early that night as well and I was devastated. That to me was the final breaking point but there are two sides of the event. This is the worst thing that happened to us, but maybe it is the best thing that had happened to us that season. Because by doing what he did made those who wanted the blue as our colour to stand up. I've noticed as the season went on and as we got to the last few games, songs about our traditional colour blue were starting to be sung.

It started with just a group of about 10 of us, while the majority of fans sung 'We're Cardiff City, we're top of the league', we sang 'We're Cardiff City, we'll always be blue.'

The final three games of the season when we went to Watford, Burnley and Hull away, that was all you could hear from the crowd, 'We'll always be blue' and 'the blues are going up'. I nearly gave up going anymore the night before the Burnley trip.

'I can't go no more...' But I am glad I still did keep going. The final two home games were against Charlton and Bolton and it was against Charlton when the fans invaded the pitch after we won promotion that night on April 17th 2012, after 51 years, something I dreamed about all my life, to go to the Premier League. I walked out of the stadium actually quite sad. Just why couldn't we be in blue?

I went back to the Ninian Park Pub and watched all those fans on the pitch. But I looked at them and thought 'Would you be there if we got relegated?' No you wouldn't. I remember when we had just 11 fans that went away at one game and it was the norm for there just to be just 50 or maybe 100.

I know their faces, I know those people. So enjoy your glory of the night, but it is not the same without our identity. Against Burnley I actually stayed to the end of the game and I did watch the celebrations as we had just won the championship.

Then I went down to our stadium for the Bolton game, it was the day we had the championship trophy presented to us. As Vincent Tan walked towards that trophy, I looked at him and I thought 'oh my god' he was covered in red. But as he got closer to the trophy to touch it, our little group started singing 'We'll always be blue' and at least 18000 fans out of nearly 27000 that day sang 'We'll always be blue'. I loved it.

I studied and stared at Tan and I could see, he stopped and his head looked up. What upset me a bit was that the stadium announcer, on the microphone saying 'can we move on, can we move on.' But 18000 fans sang 'We'll always be blue'!

We know we will not get our identity back under Tan. But what we will do is to keep reminding the youngsters that are coming through, that our true identity is blue, that we are the Bluebirds, what our badge is and should be and what our identity is.

What will we manage to achieve?

We'll manage to remind people at the stadium of who we are and we will show away fans of teams we will play in Premier League, that some of us do have pride and respect for our identity, some of us haven't sold our souls. We are broken and hurt but we are fighting back in a good way. We are fighting back without disrupting the club, without turning on the team.

I just believe that if we turn up at every

match in blue, home and away, I think we will grow... it's quite sad really that these could be the most magical moments, the best days of my life, it's been hurt by someone taking our identity away. I met the owner Vincent Tan, yes he is red through and through.

The reasons for rebrand, which he gave me personally, straight to my face, 'Red is lucky, this is the way forward, red is happiness, red is the way of world'. Sorry it doesn't wash with me, I am not convinced. Cardiff City are blue. We could have got promotion in blue. There was no reason for change. 'Red will sell more in Asia', Rubbish. Unless you win and continue to win in the Premier League, that's what sells in Asia. They only support the winning team, no such thing about colour.

We are blue and we are strong.

That's what was happening to me and fair dues to Bart. He has shown both sides of the story in this book, red and blue. I am not turning against red. That's up to those who support the re-

brand, that's their opinion; I just can't believe that people would wear it. I'm just hoping that this season we will get stronger! And I mean stronger. What is sad is that the club shop started to sell less blue merchandise. Let's hope that street traders will sell blue and that they make a fortune out of it. They deserve it, anyone who sells blue now deserves it, because our own club won't sell it.

I started supporting City in 1972 and they were blue. As far as I am concerned – they are blue now. Long live Cardiff City and the Bluebirds!

THE SEASON BY CARL CURTIS

I have supported Cardiff City since 1988 despite growing up on the doorstep of Swansea. My cousin played for the Bluebirds between 1985 and 1987 and as a result I attended my first City in an away game at Swansea and the feelings I experienced that day had such an effect I was hooked on Cardiff City.

Throughout the resulting years there was not a great deal of success and we were bouncing between the bottom two divisions of the league.

Top flight football, which eventually became the Premier League seemed an impossible dream but no matter what division Cardiff City were playing in they were my team, proud to say I supported Cardiff City whilst my mates 'supported' the likes of Man Utd and Liverpool.

At the end of the 2011/12 season we had missed out on promotion to the Premier league via the play-offs again but the season was still deemed a success on the pitch, we had a new manager, Malky Mackay, who started to rebuild the team and nothing more than a mid-table finish was expected of him in his first season.

Malky guided the team to a League Cup Final, which we narrowly lost on penalties to Liverpool, and a play-off spot, as fans we ended the season not disappointed but excited at what we could possibly achieve the following year.

The vast majority of football fans around the world read or heard about the re-branding of our club in the summer of 2012. I was not happy about it and am still not but there were too many positives attached to the re-branding of the club to drive the investor, Vincent Tan, away.

The Malaysian wanted to invest £100m and he promised to settle our debts, build a new state of the art training facility, expand our stadium, turn the £100m loan in to shares and provide the manager with significant funds to strengthen the squad for a serious attempt at gaining promotion.

We opened the Championship season live on Sky on Friday August 17th 2012 against newly promoted Huddersfield Town. Seeing the Bluebirds run out in red for the first time was surreal, it didn't look right, it didn't feel right but it was here and it was here for at least that season.

The expectation among the fans was that we would beat Huddersfield quite comfortably but that was certainly not the case, it was a dogged, resolute performance with a late winner scored in the game that became very much the story for the season, City won many of their games by the odd goal.

We were not a free flowing, fanciful footballing side who would be creating chances and scoring goals for fun but what we had was a squad that would work from the first minute until the very last, quite simply if a team were going to beat City that season they were going to have to work extremely hard to get the victory.

Our home form in the 2012/13 season was very good, the side won all of the first ten games played at Cardiff City stadium and it not until a surprise defeat to bottom of the league Peterborough on December 15th did we surrender our first point at home.

Following Cardiff City away is as much about being with fellow fans and friends as it is about following the team, the laughs we have on our trips away have often been better than the result of the actual game.

Our trips to London for an evening kick-off where we hole ourselves into a pub in Leicester Square, Clapham Junction and then 100 or so of us tube it over to Millwall, Charlton or Crystal Palace, spirits are high usually caused by the amount of alcohol consumed and the singing on a commuter packed train normally raises smiles among the locals.

By November 24th 2012, we had played four games away from home in our traditional blue but we had not recorded a win in any of the games but on that day we were away to Barnsley and despite a sending off we beat them 2-1 in our blue kit and took the top spot in the Championship which we didn't relinquish for the rest of the season.

The Christmas period is always a tough schedule for any football team, we played four games in 11 days and we won every one of them, it was at this time I genuinely believed that Cardiff City stood the best chance ever of achieving the dream.

From the turn of the year we only lost three more matches that season and with each game that passed the closer we were getting to being promoted.

As a group of regulars who travel with me on the coach trips I organise, we always look forward to the Middlesbrough away trip; we leave at 3am and are in a pub on the outskirts for around 9am, we never have any trouble at the pubs we pre-arrange and are often invited back and in most cases we usually do. Friendships have been made between people who were otherwise strangers to each other but through the football trips camaraderie has formed that will last for many years.

Highlights on the pitch for myself, were of course winning promotion against Charlton at home on April 16th 2013 but being at Burnley four days later with 1,500 other Bluebirds when we won the title will live with me forever.

We drew the game 1-1 but the celebrations were mind blowing, I reflected on what was a difficult season off the pitch for many of us because of the colour change and stripping of our identity but I wanted to celebrate the fact that we were now a Premier League club who not just got promoted but won the title as well.

It was somewhat of a bitter sweet moment for me, I would have wanted nothing more and would have felt more sense of pride had we continued to be a club who wore their traditional colour of blue but what disappointed me the most was that my eleven year old daughter, Angharad, who is at my side for every home and away game was not there to witness the historic moment.

That said thanks to Annis, who is totally opposed to the re-branding, who caught Kim Bo-Kyung's match shirt, passed it to me and gave it as a gift to her, so she will always have a piece of memorabilia from the game.

Overall the 2012/13 season was one that will forever be remembered for very different reasons. It was historic both on the pitch and off it.

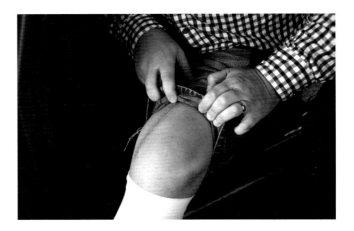

SOME THINGS HAPPEN FOR A REASON BY BARTOSZ NOWICKI

I would never have made this book but for two unexpected events which took place in August 2012. A few days out from Cardiff City FC's season opener I received an email from the German football magazine - 11 Freunde:

Hey Bartosz,

I am from the German football magazine "11 Freunde". We are looking for photographers in Wales and I see that you have studied in Newport.
Are you now in Wales or Cardiff?

Please answer very quick because we want to make a photo report in Cardiff in two days.

Best regards from Berlin.

Paul Lehr

Within hours I was assigned to photograph the inauguration of the new 'red' kit at Cardiff City Stadium and the protests that were supposed to happen just before the kick-off. The editors of 11 Freunde had seen my pictures from the stadium on Bulgarska Street (the home of Lech Poznan) and asked me to deliver images capturing a similar passion. The protest never materialised so instead I made a few images in the pubs around Canton. I worked together with Titus Chalk, a journalist who's words I was illustrating, interviewing and photographing both 'blue' and 'red' fans. Naturally these pictures were not enough so I went to the stadium to buy a ticket for the game. This is where the second event occurred. I chose a seat on the Ninian Stand, where I shot photographs during the first half. Here I met Annis Abraham Jnr., a publisher and a writer with whom I exchanged contact details. I didn't know at the time that this meeting would be the beginning of my long-term adventure with Cardiff City FC.

When the magazine came out I contacted Annis to thank him for the help he had given me during that first day at the CCS and to show him the spreads from the magazine. That day, during our email exchange I decided to continue my work with the fans. I asked Annis if they would be interested in participating in a long-term project. He said yes and this is when the gates to the heart of CCFC (which for me the supporters are) opened in front of me. Before I knew it I was following City to both home and away fixtures.

My first trip was Charlton away. To be honest I didn't know what kind of welcome to expect getting onto the Forum Bus (later renamed Carlos Coaches). Usually it takes some time for people to get used to me, and more importantly my camera. But the welcome I received on that day was overwhelming. The match itself was a weird one with the Bluebirds giving away their 2:0 lead, to be brutalised 2:5 and finally losing 4:5. Off the pitch the comradeship I witnessed on that trip will stay with me forever. On this escapade to London in October 2012 I met many characters that have become a focal point of this book, and more importantly my mates.

As the season progressed I grew more and more attached to CCFC and got to know more and more people. By the end of it I couldn't take more than a few steps towards the Ninian Pub (now The Maverick) or to the ground without bumping into one of my mates. It is a constant joy, the football day, but as much as I enjoyed the home games I felt the atmosphere at CCS wasn't the greatest (aside from the last few games of the season).

For sure there are many possible rea-sons for this, but it felt to me like it was the off-pitch situation that was the most disturbing factor of what was, in the eyes of many, the 'Bluebirds' great-est ever season. Maybe this is why I just loved the away trips? The atmosphere elsewhere always seemed to be bet-ter than at home... If I remember cor-rectly it was at Watford where I heard, for the first time, my favourite chant of the season – 'The Blues are going up!' We have been singing it relentlessly at every match since. When I look back at that championship winning season I can't stop myself from thinking about how lucky I was as a photographer to have been able to witness and record it for future generations. I can't stop myself thinking of how grateful I am to you, the Bluebirds, for letting me share it with you. It was a rollercoaster ride all the way!

As I write this Cardiff City FC are strug-gling in the promised land of the pre-mier league. There is even more off-pitch drama surrounding the club. I often wonder where CCFC will be this time next year? Naturally there is no answer to that, as only time will tell. There is however one thing I know for sure… I'll be there, surrounded by my fellow fans, with my camera to docu-ment it.

BLUEEEEEEEEBIIIIIRDS!

SUPPORTERS

Chiara Tocci, Jon Candy, Michael Hodgkinson, Dale Fisher, Phillip M Berndsen, Laura Som, Chris Anderson, James MDR Davis, Claire Kern, Ken Grant, Michal Iwanowski, Grzegorz Jaworski, Mallo Cardiff, Ashley John Jones, Nips, Tom Bradley, Lukasz Kubicki, Mark Sexton, Ewa Nowicka, Mad Lou, Chris Parsons, Mr Andrew Evans, Christopher Meirick, Stephen Guy a.k.a. Troobloo3339, William Davis Guy, Stevie Guy, Martyn Moses, Wayne David, Mike Thomas, Richard Boucher, Lee Spear, Jason Lewis, Martyn Tobin, Will Voyce, Luca Eckley, Louise Alana Jones, Dai Leek, Daniel Bradford, Will Hartley, Michael Rossiter, Glenn Edwards, Steven 'Nukes' Thomas, John Coleman, Stephen Williams, Magda Gibczynska, Cameron Pocock, Michael Pocock, Alan Pocock, Damion "JAFFA" Jefferies, Charles Kirk, Richard Huw Morgan, John McKernan, Paul 'The Chief' Ferrel, Cerri Young, Janire Najera, Daniel Mason, Simon Mccarthy, Evan Press, Mansel Carter, Alan Parsons, Jonathan Pratt, Dane Collett, Jimmy 'The Jock', Enzo De Vincenzo, Michael Pakes, The Doc, Millie Patterson, Leigh Evans, Mark Walby, Liam Fisher, Barrie Thomas, Keith David Evans, Neil 'Peely' Evans, Brian Armour, Mr & Mrs Prendergast, Chunk, Kacie Hall, Fedele Napolitano, David Cannon, Carwyn Thomas, Francesco Loreto, Dibs, Uros Rajkovic (Partizan Belgrade), Andrea Cavaliere, Magdalena Garczynska, Danilo Foglia, Nicola Baker, Russell Curtis, Anthonie Casey, Leigh C James, Paul Beard, Stuart Beard, James Beard, Mark Hasson, John 'Simmo' Simmonds, ABC Foto Stęszew, Joanne Abraham, Annaise Abraham, Alexandra Abraham, Tilly Abraham, Dave Bennett, Bobby McCluskie (Scotch Corner/Chili Bites Mallorca), Steve Russell (Scottish Corner/Santa Ponsa), Mason Edwards (Santa Ponsa), Mikey Hamilton (Santa Ponsa), Tony Tointon (Kensighton Pub/Santa Ponsa). Jim Leighton, Alex Leighton, Barry Hobson, Neil Wilkie, Alice Watkins, Steve Luke, Anthony Keegan, Charlotte Watkins, Jonny Griffiths, Giles Watkins, Grant Fisher, Robin Mitchell, Peter Evans, Cameron Curtis, Aaron Curtis, Angharad Curtis, Alison Hope, Jamie Curtis, Paul Wright, Huw Spickett, Mark Spickett, Gareth Parfitt, Andy 'Pealo' Jones, James Murray, Luton 'Jules' Bluebird, David Jenkins, Tim Wood, Catherine Sharples, Steve 'Horse' Jones, Liv Jones, Gideon Marchant, Steve Hatton.

THANK YOU

Thank you Baby for your patience, especially in this last, crazy month.

Annis Abrahan Jnr, without your help and contacts the making of this project wouldn't have been possible and this is only the tip of the iceberg of the things you have done to help in the creation of this record. Stephen Guy, your support in bringing this book to reality was simply great, you are a true gentlemen and are always thinking of others. Gaspare Coscarella, you are the best designer I personally know. Carl Curtis and James Leighton I thank you for your thoughts on what the season meant to you. And Mallo, for the good word from the early stages of making this project to the sponsoring of my first solo exhibition.

Thank you to 11 Freunde for the job that started it all (some things happen for a reason). Thank you to all Carlos Coaches crew for the great time we all had together and for accepting me in your ranks. Thanks to everyone who allowed me to photograph them, it's been a privilege. Claire Kern, your help along the way was crucial; no matter if it was printing, lending equipment - you name it. Paul Corcoran for being my text editor since forever now! Gareth Owen for text support and the PR that also ended up on the back cover of this book. Thank you to Gareth 'Think Big' Phillips, Chiara Tocci, Gawain Barnard, Ken Grant, Richard Huw Morgan, Simon Gaskell, Joni Karanka, Maciej Dakowicz, Robert Kennedy (perfect timing), Timothy Nordhoff, Daniel Mason, Peter Evans. Thank you to Dimitra Kontiou for equipment support at the early stages of the project. Thank you to everyone on the list of supporters of this book, you made the printing of this book possible.

Thank you David Hurn, it is an hounor to know you, you are a true inspiration.

I dedicate this book to my family.

CAPTIONS

p.4-5 › 06.11.2012 Charlton Athletic FC - Cardiff City FC.
A few hours before kick-off, the CCFC supporters on their way to a pub in Leicester Square, London.

p.6 › 27.10.2012 - Cardiff City FC - Burnley FC (after the game).
The Bluebird had been the Cardiff City FC symbol for almost a century. And the team's colour was blue. At the beginning of the 2012-13 season, the club's majority owner, Malaysian businessman Vincent Tan, introduced its change to red. His decision divided the fans and stirred an identity crisis.

p.9 › 17.08.2012 - Cardiff City FC - Huddersfield Town AFC.
The home match against Huddersfield saw the red kit make its first appearance.

p.10-11 › 04.04.2013 - Burnley FC - Cardiff City FC.
David Marshall in action at Burnley, where City clinched the championship title.

p.12 ›17.08.2012 - Cardiff City FC - Huddersfield Town AFC.
The home match against Huddersfield saw the red kit make its first appearance.

p.13-14 ›17.08.2012 - Cardiff City FC - Huddersfield Town AFC.
Scarves.

p.15 ›17.11.2012 - Cardiff City FC - Middlesbrough FC.
Annis Abraham Jnr watches the home game against Middlesbrough.

p.20 › 27.11.2012 - Derby County FC - Cardiff City FC.
Pride Park Stadium, Derby.

p.21 ›28.02.2012 - Vincent Tan interviewed by BBC.
First public interview with the Malaysian owner of CCFC. In the interview VT shares his hopes for the club's popularity in Asia and calls the local fans 'customers'. The term, seen as controversial in the culture of football, caused uproar in the local supporters' community.

p.22 ›02.02.2013 - Cardiff City FC - Leeds United AFC.
Frazier Campbell became one of the fans' favourites at Elland Road after the away game at Leeds.

p.23 › 13.11.2012 - Cardiff City FC – Swansea City AFC (development game).
Kadeem Harris leaves the ground during the development team match versus arch rivals - Swansea City AFC.

p.24 ›24.02.2013 – Wolverhampton Wanderers FC - Cardiff City FC.
City supporters at the Molineux Stadium.

p.25 › 04.05.2013 – Hull City AFC – Cardiff City FC.
CCFC had secured their championship title before the last game of the season. For City fans the trip to Hull was an occasion to cel-

ebrate. Many fans wore costumes.

p.26 › 16.02.2013 - Cardiff City FC - Bristol City FC.
After the game, the away supporters are escorted to the train station by the police.

p.27 ›04.05.2013 – Hull City AFC – Cardiff City FC.
Stephen Guy getting ready for the away trip to Hull. CCFC had secured their championship title before the last game of the season. For City fans the trip was an occasion to celebrate. Steve went as Han Solo.

p.28 › 02.03.2013 - Middlesbrough FC - Cardiff City FC.
Steve Guy plays with his grandson William on the way to Middlesbrough.

p.29 › 06.04.2013 - Watford FC - Cardiff City FC.
Gaining one point against Watford was another step closer to promotion. Cardiff City fans wait for their buses and the journey home.

p.30 ›27.04.2013 - Cardiff City FC - Bolton Wanderers FC.
Matt Connolly in action.

p.32 ›03.11.2012 - Bolton Wanderers FC - Cardiff City FC.
City fans watching the game in the Corporation Pub in Canton.

p.33 › 04.05.2013 – Hull City AFC – Cardiff City FC.
Mad Lou's tattoo.

p.34 › 04.04.2013 - Burnley FC - Cardiff City FC.
On the bus on the way to Burnley.

p.34 › 02.03.2013 - Middlesbrough FC - Cardiff City FC.
English Cardiff City FC fan, before the game in Middlesbrough.

p.35 ›02.02.2013 - Cardiff City FC - Leeds United AFC.
Frazier Campbell became one of the fans' favourites at Elland Road after the away game at Leeds.

p.36 › 23.10.2012 - Cardiff City FC - Watford FC.
Losing goal against Watford.

p.40 › 06.04.2013 - Watford FC - Cardiff City FC.
Paul Cummings, a Bluebird from Scotland, watches the game at Vicarage Road.

p.41 › 16.04.2013 – Cardiff City FC - Charlton Athletic FC.
Pitch invasion after the Bluebirds secured their promotion to the Premier League.

p.42 › 06.04.2013 - Watford FC - Cardiff City FC.
Police patrol after the game at Vicarage Road.

p.43 › 06.11.2012 - Charlton Athletic FC - Cardiff City FC.
'Chief' on the train to Charlton.

05.01.2012 - Macclesfield Town FC – Cardiff City FC.
Dan Bradford shows his tattoo in a pub in Macclesfield.

02.02.2013 - Cardiff City FC - Leeds United AFC.
Steve Scaccia on the bus to Leeds.

p.44 › 09.01.2013 - Huddersfield Town AFC – Cardiff City FC.
On the way to Huddersfield, Mallo shares a story of a trip to Croatia with Pokey and others.

p.45 › 09.01.2013 - Huddersfield Town AFC – Cardiff City FC.
City fans at a pub in Rochdale, during a stop on the way to Huddersfield.

p.46 › 19.02.2013 - Cardiff City FC - Brighton & Hove Albion FC (before the game).
The day of the red scarves give away.
The Fred Keenor statue was erected earlier in the season, thanks to the work of the Cardiff City SupportersTrust.

p. 46 › 06.11.2012 - Charlton Athletic FC - Cardiff City FC.
Sharing a laugh on the way to London.

p.47 › 05.03.2013 - Cardiff City FC – Derby County FC.
'Dibs' watches the home game against Derby.

p.48 › 16.04.2013 – Cardiff Bay, Parade of Champions.
Craig Bellamy with the trophy.

p.49 ›04.04.2013 - Burnley FC - Cardiff City FC.
'Fishy' after the final whistle of the game at Burnley where CCFC clinched the championship title.

p.50-51 › 26.04.2013 - Cardiff, Holland House Hotel.
A day before his first ever visit to Cardiff City Stadium, Sam Hammam met with Cardiff City fans at the Holland House Hotel. Hammam, who represented Langston and their loan notes, arrived in Cardiff to discuss the settlement of the historical 'Langston Debt' with Vincent Tan.

p.52 › 28.04.2013 - Treforest, Cardiff City FC Academy.
Sunday morning after the first team's game vs Bolton, Vincent Tan and Sam Hammam met again to watch the CCFC youngsters at the Academy. Later that year the 'Langston Debt' was settled.

p.55 ›11.06.2013 – Corporation Pub, Cardiff.
Sian Branson, the founder of Bluebirds Unite, at the Corporation Pub during their second gathering. BU, a group run by fans, became the only organised opposition to the club re-branding.